Creamy Chicken 12

Ratatouille Chickpeas 15

Slow Cooker Fajitas 18

Slow Duck Breast 21

Slow Cooker Herb Potatoes 23

Squash Casserole 26

Caribbean Stew 29

Slow Cooked Scalloped Golden Potatoes 32

Black Bean Soup 34

Honey Sriracha Wings 37

Corn and Potato Chowder 40

French Onion Soup 43

Slow Cooker Roasted Vegetables 46

Vegetable Mix 49

Vermicelli with Rice 52

Quinoa with Cherries 55

Sweet Pineapple Chicken 57

Slow Cooker

Anti – Inflammatory Recipes

Includes: 2 Anti – Inflammation

Diet Recipes Books

75+ Recipes

Cindy Myers

Recipe Junkies

Thank you for ordering this anti – inflammatory recipe book. This book contains 2 books in one! 75+ delicious, anti – inflammatory recipes to choose from.

Enjoy!

White Bean Soup 194

Turkey stew 197

Crock Beans 200

Vegetable and Cheese Soup 202

Vegetable and Black Bean Soup 204

Bowtie Pasta and Homemade Tomato Sauce 206

Rice Casserole 208

Potato Soup 210

Split Pea Soup 212

Onion Soup 214

Zucchini Soup 216

German Lentil Soup 218

Meatless Taco Soup 220

Cabbage Soup 222

Corn Chowder 224

Tofu Curry 226

Anti – Inflammation

Diet Recipes

Slow Cooker

Anti – Inflammatory Recipes

Cindy Myers

Recipe Junkies

Large print edition.

Many of our subscribers, and readers ask for large print editions of our recipe books, and recipe books we promote of others. We hope you enjoy this large print edition of these recipes. Be sure to view the eBook version of this book, or the free preview. Click the links to our pages, and mailing lists, for delicious recipes!

Reviews are always appreciated, and we thank you in advance. Enjoy!

Creamy Chicken

Serves 3 - 6

Ingredients:

3 lbs of Chicken Breast – Boneless, Skinless

1 Package of Italian Salad Dressing Mix

1 Small Onion - Chopped

1 Clove of Garlic- Chopped

1 Can of Cream of Chicken Soup

8 Ounces of Low Fat Cream Cheese

½ Cup of Chicken Broth

1 tbsp coconut oil

1 tsp cayenne pepper

Instructions:

Lightly oil bottom of pot.

Place your chicken in your crock-pot, and then sprinkle the Italian seasoning, and cayenne pepper on the chicken.

Cook it on the low setting for 4-6 hours, with a small amount of water. Sauté the onions and the garlic with coconut oil. Add the Cream of Chicken Soup, the low fat cream cheese, as well as the chicken broth. Stir it until it is smooth.

Add the mix to your crock-pot. Cook on the low setting for an added hour.

Nutritional Information per serving:

Calories: 547

Total Fat: 44g

Saturated Fat: 19g

Carbohydrates: 6g

Protein: 29g

Ratatouille Chickpeas

Serves 3 - 5

Ingredients:

1 Tablespoon of Olive Oil

1 Red Onion - Chopped

4 Garlic Cloves - Minced

6 Cup of Eggplants - Cubed

2 Teaspoons of Basil

1 Teaspoon of Oregano

½ Teaspoons of Salt

½ Teaspoons of pepper

1 Red Bell Pepper

1 Yellow Bell Pepper

2 Green Zucchinis

⅓ Cups of Tomato Paste

1 Can of Chickpeas- Drained, Rinsed

1 Can of Tomatoes

¼ Cup of Fresh Basil Chopped

Instructions:

In a large pan, heat the oil on medium, cook your onions, the garlic, the eggplant, the basil, oregano, and the salt and pepper, stirring sporadically until the onion is softened, approximately 10 minutes. Put it into the crockpot. Halve, core, and then seed the peppers; cut them into 1-inch pieces. Cut the zucchini into halves lengthwise, and then cut them crosswise into 1 1/2-inch pieces. Add it to the Slow Cooker.

Add tomato paste, chickpeas, and tomatoes, breaking up tomatoes with a spoon. Cover and cook on low for 4 hours, or until vegetables are tender. Stir in basil.

Nutritional Information per Serving:

Calories: 219

Total Fat: 37g

Saturated Fat: 1g

Carbohydrates: 40g

Protein: 9g

Slow Cooker Fajitas

Serves 2 - 3

Ingredients:

1 Red Bell Pepper

1 Yellow Bell Pepper

1 Green Bell Pepper

1 White Onion

1 Packet Taco or Fajita Seasoning

1 Pound of Chicken Breasts –
Boneless, Skinless

½ Cup of Chicken Broth

Toppings - Low Fat Vegan Cheese,
Low Fat Vegan Sour Cream, or
Salsa(optional)

Whole Grain Tortillas

Instructions:

Slice the bell peppers and the onions in ¼ inch pieces. Add them to the bottom of your slow cooker. Sprinkle the taco or fajita seasoning on the bell peppers and the onions in your slow cooker. Add in the chicken breasts and the chicken broth. Cook it on the low setting for 6-8 hours.

Remove the chicken from the Crockpot and let cool slightly. Use two forks to shred the chicken. Add shredded chicken back to Crockpot and mix with peppers and onions. Serve over/with tortillas or alone with your choice of toppings (like cheese, salsa, guacamole, sour cream, fresh cilantro).

Nutritional Information per Serving:

Calories: 335

Total Fat: 12g

Carbohydrates: 41g

Protein: 19g

Slow Duck Breast

Serves 2 - 4

Ingredients:

2 Whole Wild Duck Breasts – Halved, Skin Removed

1/2 Teaspoons of Salt

1/4 Teaspoon of Black Pepper

2 Small Oranges – Peeled, Cut into 1/2-inch Pieces

1 Medium Apple - Cut into 1/2-inch pieces

1 Medium Onion - Cut into Eighths

(6 Ounces) Frozen Orange Juice

Spice mix seasoning (optional)

Instructions:

Sprinkle the duck with salt and pepper. Layer the duck, the oranges, the apples and the onions in a 3 1/2 - 6 quart slow cooker. Pour the orange juice concentrate on the top. Cover it and cook it on the low setting for 8-10 hours.

Remove the duck from cooker and discard the fruit and the onion mixture.

Nutritional Information per Serving:

Calories: 246

Total Fat: 4g

Saturated Fat: 1g

Carbohydrates: 32g

Protein: 18g

Slow Cooker Herb Potatoes

Serves 3 - 4

Ingredients:

6 Medium Golden potatoes

¼ Cups of Water

1 Teaspoon of Salt

1 Teaspoon of Pepper

1 Teaspoon of Garlic Powder

1 Teaspoon of Minced White Onion

½ Teaspoons of Dried Dill

1 Teaspoon of Italian Seasoning

1 Teaspoon of Parsley

4 Tablespoon of Coconut Oil

Instructions:

Chop your potatoes into half-moons (slice the potatos in half the long-ways, then to pieces). Place them into the slow cooker. Add the water and then sprinkle it with all the herbs and the seasoning. Stir it to distribute the herbs evenly.

Add the oil on the top of your potatoes.

Cover it and cook it on the low setting for 5 hours.

Nutritional Information per serving:

Calories: 353

Total Fat: 11g

Saturated Fat: 7g

Carbohydrates: 57g

Protein: 7g

Squash Casserole

Serves 3 - 4

Ingredients:

9 Cups of Sliced Yellow Summer Squash (5 Medium Squashes)

1 Medium Sweet Onion - Chopped

1 Tablespoon Coconut Oil

2 Cups of French Bread Crumbs

8 Ounces of Shredded Sharp Cheddar Cheese

2/3 Cups of Low Fat Sour Cream

½ Teaspoon of Garlic Salt

¼ Teaspoon of Pepper

1 Can (10 3/4 oz) Condensed Cream of

Chicken Soup

Chopped Fresh Parsley

Instructions:

Non Stick spray a 5- to 6-quart slow

cooker. In your slow cooker, mix in

the squash mixture, 8 ounces of the

breadcrumbs, and 1/2 cup of the

cheese, the low fat sour cream, the

garlic salt, the pepper and the soup.

In small bowl, mix remaining 8

ounces of breadcrumbs, remaining 1/2

cup of cheese and the oil. Sprinkle the

crumb mixture over squash.

Cover it and then cook it on the low setting for 2 hours. Uncover it and remove the insert from your slow cooker. Let it stand for 30 minutes before serving. Sprinkle with parsley, if desired.

Nutritional Information per Serving:

Calories: 180

Total Fat: 12g

Saturated Fat: 6g

Carbohydrates: 12g

Protein: 5g

Caribbean Stew

Serves 3 - 5

Ingredients:

2 Medium Sweet Potatoes

2 Chicken Breast Halves – Boneless

½ lb vegan sausage (optional)

1 Large Red Onion - Chopped

2 Cloves of Garlic - Finely Minced

1 Can of Whole Tomatoes with Juice

1 Can of Garbanzo Beans - Drained

1 Teaspoon of Paprika

1 Teaspoon of Salt

1 Teaspoon of Thyme

1 Teaspoon of Ground Black Pepper

1/2 Teaspoons of Allspice

1/2 Teaspoons of Cumin

2 Tablespoons of Tomato Paste

Chopped Parsley

Instructions:

Peel and then dice the sweet potatoes into 1-inch cubes. Cut the chicken and the sausage into 1-inch pieces.

In your slow cooker, combine the sweet potatoes, your chicken, onion, sausage, garlic, tomatoes, paprika, beans, pepper, thyme, salt, allspice, the cumin, and the tomato paste. Cover it and allow it to simmer on the low setting until the sweet potatoes are tender, approximately 4 hours.

To serve it ladle it into bowls and garnish it with parsley.

Nutritional Information per Serving:

Calories: 336

Total Fat: 10g

Saturated Fat: 3g

Carbohydrates: 30g

Protein: 30g

Slow Cooked Scalloped Golden Potatoes

Serves 4 -6

Ingredients:

3 Pounds of Yukon Gold Potatoes – Unpeeled, Thinly Sliced

1 Large Onion - Thinly Sliced

1/2 Cups of Cashew Milk

1/2 Cups of Vegan Parmesan Cheese

1/2 Teaspoons of Salt

1/4 Teaspoon of Black Pepper

Directions:

Spray your 6-quart slow cooker with cooking spray. Layer 1/3 of your potatoes and ½ of the onions in your cooker. Repeat layers. Top it with the rest of the potatoes.

Stir in the milk, cheese, salt, and the black pepper in a bowl. Cover it and cook it on the high setting for 4-5 hours.

Sprinkle it with more cheese if desired. Cover it and allow it to stand for 5 minutes.

Nutritional Information per Serving:

Calories: 370   Total Fat: 11g

Carbohydrates: 46g

Protein: 12g

Black Bean Soup

Serves 2- 3

Ingredients:

2 Cloves of Garlic

1 Medium White Onion

2 Stalks of Celery

2 Medium Carrots

1 lb. of Black Beans - Uncooked

8 Ounces of Salsa

1 Tablespoon of Chili Powder

½ Tablespoon of Cumin

1 Tablespoon of Oregano

4 Cups of Vegetable Broth

2 Cups of Water

Instructions:

Mince the garlic, dice the onions, as well as the celery. Grate your carrots on a large cheese grater. Rinse the black beans using a colander under cold water and pick out any debris. Combine the garlic, your onion, the celery, black beans, carrots, salsa, chili powder, oregano, cumin, the vegetable broth, and the water in your 5-7 quart cooker. Stir it well.

Place the lid on your slow cooker and then cook it on the high setting for 6-8 hours. Once the beans are soft, blend in the soup until it's thick.

Nutritional Information per Serving:

Calories: 134

Total Fat: 1g

Saturated Fat: 1g

Carbohydrates: 19g

Protein: 6g

Honey Sriracha Wings

Serves 4 - 8

Ingredients:

4 Pounds of Chicken Wings - Frozen

3/4 Cups of Sriracha Sauce

3/4 Cups of Honey

2 Tablespoons of Unsalted Butter (or Coconut Oil)

Juice of One Lime

Instructions:

Add the sriracha, honey, butter, and lime juice. Stir in to combine. Add in the chicken wings. Stir it until the wings are well coated. Cook them on the low setting for 6-8 hours or on the high setting for 3-4 hours. Remove the wings from your slow cooker and then place them on a baking sheet that is lined with foil. Drizzle on the sauce from the cooker on the wings.

Set your oven to broil. Place the baking sheet inside the oven and bake them for 2-3 minutes. Remove them from the oven.

Nutritional Information per Serving:

Calories: 351

Total Fat: 15g

Saturated Fat: 2g

Carbohydrates: 19g

Protein: 35g

Corn and Potat Chowder

Serves 4 - 6

Ingredients:

24 Ounces of Red Potatoes - Diced

1 (16-ounce) Package of Frozen

Corn

3 Tablespoon of Coconut Flour

6 Cups of Chicken Stock

1 Teaspoon of Dried Thyme

1 Teaspoon of Dried Oregano

1/2 Teaspoons of Garlic Powder

1/2 Teaspoons of Onion Powder

Salt and Black Pepper

2 Tablespoons of Unsalted Butter

1/4 Cups of Heavy Cream

Instructions:

Place the potatoes and the corn into your slow cooker. Stir in the flour and toss it to combine it. Stir in the chicken stock, the thyme, garlic powder, oregano, onion powder, salt and pepper.

Cover it and cook it on the low setting for 7-8 hours or high heat for 3-4 hours. Stir in the butter and the heavy cream.

Serve it immediately.

Nutritional Information per Serving:

Calories: 384

Total Fat: 144g

Saturated Fat: 5g

Carbohydrates: 54g

Protein: 9g

French Onion Soup

Serves 6 - 10

Ingredients:

1/4 Cup of Butter

6 Thyme Sprigs

1 Bay Leaf

5 Pounds of Sweet Onions - Vertically Sliced

6 Cups of Vegetable Stock

2 Tablespoons of Red Wine Vinegar

1 1/2 Teaspoons of Salt

1 Teaspoon of Black Pepper

12 Slices Whole-Grain French Bread

5 Ounces of Gruyère Cheese -
Shredded

Instructions:

1. Place the butter, thyme, and the bay leaf in the bottom of your 6-quart slow cooker. Add in the onions. Cover it and cook then cook it on the high setting for 8 hours.

2. Remove the thyme and the bay leaf; discard it. Add in the stock, vinegar, the salt, and some pepper; cook it covered on the high setting for 30 minutes.

3. Preheat your broiler to high.

4. Arrange the bread in a single layer; broil it for 30 seconds on each side. Serve on side.

Nutritional Information per Serving:

Calories: 240

Total Fat: 8g

Saturated Fat: 3g

Carbohydrates: 33g

Protein: 9g

Slow Cooker Roasted Vegetables

Serves 2 - 4

Ingredients:

4 Russet Potatoes – Chopped, Large Pieces

2 Carrots

1/2 Sweet Onion - Sliced

2 Zucchinis - Thickly Sliced

Olive Oil

1 Packet of Dry Italian Dressing Mix

Instructions:

Place the chopped vegetables in a bowl

Drizzle the vegetables with the olive oil.

Sprinkle the packet of Italian seasoning on the vegetables.

Lightly toss it so all of the vegetables are covered in oil and the seasoning.

Spray the slow cooker with non-stick spray and dump the seasoned vegetables in.

Cook it on the low setting for 5-7 hours or on the high setting for 3-4 hours.

Nutritional Information per serving:

Calories: 193

Total Fat: 5g

Saturated Fat: 1g

Carbohydrates: 32g

Protein: 3g

Vegetable Mix

Serves: 4 -7

Ingredients:

1 medium carrot, peeled and cut into small pieces

2 medium golden potato, peeled and diced into cubes

1 large white onion, chopped

2 large tomatoes, chopped

1 cup coriander leaves, chopped

2 garlic clove, minced

1 tablespoon grated ginger

4 tablespoons olive oil

1 teaspoon pepper

1 teaspoon cumin

5 cups water

2 teaspoons salt

Directions:

1. Take a saucepan and heat olive oil in pan.

2. Add onion, ginger, garlic and carrots in pan and stir-fry for 5 minutes over medium heat.

3. Add tomatoes, potatoes and chopped coriander then stir-fry for further 5 minutes.

4. Add remaining ingredients and bring to boil.

5. Cover pan with lid and simmer over medium-low heat for 60 minutes. Add more water if necessary.

6. Puree soup with blender until completely smooth.

7. Serve hot and enjoy.

Nutritional Information per Serving:

Calories 125

Fat 7.3 g

Saturated Fat 1 g

Carbohydrates 14.7 g

Protein 2 g

Vermicelli with Rice

Serves: 2 - 4

Ingredients:

1 cup white rice, rinsed

1/2 cup thin vermicelli, cut into small

pieces

2 cups water

4 tablespoons butter

1/4 teaspoon cinnamon

1/4 teaspoon pepper

3/4 teaspoon salt

Directions:

1. In a pan, add butter when butter melted adds vermicelli and sauté until the vermicelli pieces begin to turn golden brown.

2. Add rice in pan and stir-fry for 2 minutes.

3. Add remaining ingredients in pan except cinnamon, and then bring to boil.

4. Cover pan with lid and cook over low heat for 10 minutes.

5. Turn off heat and stir. Recover with lid and allow to cook in own steam for 25 minutes.

6. Place in serving bowl and sprinkle with cinnamon and serve with vegetable stew.

Nutritional Information per Serving:

Calories 271

Fat 11.8 g

Saturated Fat 7.4 g

Carbohydrates 37.2 g

Protein 3.4 g

Quinoa with Cherries

Serves: 3 - 6

Ingredients:

2 cups quinoa, rinsed and drained

2 cups almonds

2 cups dried cherries

6 cups Almond milk

Pinch of salt

Directions:

8. Add quinoa, almonds, cherries, milk and salt in slow cooker.

9. Mix all ingredients gently.

10. Cover slow cooker with lid and cook on low for 8 hours.

Nutritional Information per Serving:

Calories 385

Fat 18.2 g

Saturated Fat 3.5 g

Carbohydrates 41.4 g

Sugar 9.2 g

Protein 17 g

Sweet Pineapple Chicken

Serves: 3 - 4

Ingredients:

1 cup broccoli florets

1 cup yellow and red bell pepper, chopped

2 chicken breasts, boneless and skinless

4 ounce canned pineapple chunks with juice

5 ounce sweet chili salsa

Directions:

1. Place chicken in slow cooker and pour pineapple chunks and chili sauce over the chicken.

2. Cook on low for 5 hours. About 1 hour before of serving slice the chicken and stir back into the sauce.

3. Place broccoli and bell pepper on top of the chicken mixture and cook until vegetable are tender.

4. Serve hot with rice and enjoy.

Nutritional Information per Serving:

Calories 210

Fat 3 g

Saturated Fat 0 g

Carbohydrates 20.2 g

Protein 20 g

Pumpkin Soup

Serves: 3 - 5

Ingredients:

2 cups pumpkin puree

1/4 cup yellow bell pepper, chopped

1 white onion, chopped

2 cups chicken stock

1 teaspoon parsley, chopped

1/4 cup water

1/4 teaspoon nutmeg

1/8 teaspoon thyme, dried

2 cups plain Almond milk

1/2 teaspoon salt

Directions:

1. Add pumpkin puree, bell pepper, onion, chicken stock, nutmeg, thyme, milk and salt in slow cooker and combine well.

2. Cover cooker with a lid and cook on low for 4 hours.

3. Mix until soup becomes thick.

4. Garnish with parsley and serve hot.

Nutritional Information per Serving:

Calories 173

Fat 3 g

Saturated Fat 0 g

Carbohydrates 23 g

Protein 8 g

Slow Cooker Chickpea

Serves: 3 - 4

Ingredients:

1/2 cup dried chickpeas, soak overnight

1 teaspoon olive oil

1 small onion, chopped

1/8 teaspoon cinnamon

1/2 tablespoon ginger paste

1/2 teaspoon cayenne

1/2 teaspoon asafetida powder

1/2 teaspoon coriander

1/2 teaspoon turmeric

1/2 tablespoon cumin

1 tablespoon tomato paste

1 small tomato, chopped

Water as needed

Directions:

1. In a small, pan heat olive oil and add chopped onion, ginger and garlic and sauté until onion becomes soften.

2. Add chickpeas in slow cooker. Now add onion mixture in slow cooker and mix well.

3. Then add remaining ingredients and stir well.

4. Cook on low for 8 hours.

5. Stir well before serving.

Nutritional Information per Serving:

Calories 144

Fat 3 g

Saturated Fat 0 g

Carbohydrates 19 g

Protein 5.7 g

Vegetables with Tofu

Serves: 4 - 6

Ingredients:

2 cups cabbage, chopped

2 cups bok Choy, chopped

1/2 cup celery, chopped

1/2 cup onion, chopped

16 ounce firm tofu, crumbled

Directions:

1. Combine all ingredients in slow cooker. Cover with lid and cook on low for 6 hours.

2. Stir well before serving. Serve with rice and enjoy.

Nutritional Information per Serving:

Calories 82

Fat 3 g

Saturated Fat 0 g

Carbohydrates 4 g

Sugar 2 g

Protein 7 g

Lemon Potatoes

Serves: 3 - 5

Ingredients:

2 pounds small golden potatoes

3 tablespoon fresh chives, snipped

1 tablespoon lemon juice

2 tablespoon coconut oil

1/4 cup water

1/2 teaspoon black pepper

1 teaspoon salt

Fresh parsley, chopped

Directions:

1. Make a cut of strip around the middle of each potato.

2. Place potatoes in slow cooker and pour water over.

3. Cover slow cooker with lid and cook on high for 3 hours.

4. Drain potatoes completely.

5. Combine chives, lemon juice, oil and parsley.

6. Pour the oil mixture over the potatoes and toss well until coated.

7. Season with pepper and salt.

Serve immediately and enjoy.

Nutritional Information per Serving:

Calories 180

Fat 3.8 g

Saturated Fat 2.1 g

Carbohydrates 31 g

Protein 3 g

Kidney and Black Beans Chili

Serves: 4 - 6

Ingredients:

15 ounces canned kidney beans, rinsed and drained

1 cup corn kernels

15 ounces canned black beans, rinsed and drained

1 teaspoon cumin

2 teaspoon jalapeno hot sauce

1 teaspoon paprika

1 teaspoon chili powder

1 teaspoon cayenne

3 garlic cloves, minced

1 onion, chopped

2 carrots, diced

2 celery stalks, diced

25 ounces canned tomatoes, diced

1 teaspoon jalapeno, minced

Directions:

1. Add all ingredients in slow cooker except corn.

2. Cover cooker with lid and cook on low for 6 hours.

3. Stir well and add corn kernels. Cover the cooker again and cook on low for 1 hour.

4. Serve hot and enjoy.

Nutritional Information per Serving:

Calories 340

Fat 2.5 g

Saturated Fat 0 g

Carbohydrates 48 g

Protein 33 g

White Bean Soup

Serves: 3 - 4

Ingredients:

14 ounce canned white beans,

rinsed and drained

3 cups vegetable stock

14 ounce canned tomatoes

crushed, drained

1 onion, diced

1 carrot, diced

2 celery stalks, diced

1 garlic cloves, minced

2 tablespoon olive oil

Pepper

Salt

Directions:

1. In small pan, heat olive oil over medium heat and add onion, carrot, garlic and celery sauté until vegetables are soften.

2. Now add tomatoes in pan and combine well.

3. Transfer vegetable mixture into the slow cooker.

4.Add white beans and vegetable stock in cooker.

5. Close cooker with lid and cook on low for 6 hours.

6.Season with pepper and salt and serve hot.

Nutritional Information per Serving:

Calories 240

Fat 7.9 g

Saturated Fat 1.2 g

Carbohydrates 34 g

Protein 13 g

Eggplant

Serves: 3 - 6

Ingredients:

- 2 tablespoon olive oil
- 8 ounce vegan cheese, crumbled
- 32 ounce marinara sauce
- 1/2 cup basil, chopped
- 1 large eggplant, sliced
- 1 yellow squash, sliced
- 1 large zucchini, sliced
- 1 onion, sliced
- 2 green bell peppers, sliced

Directions:

1. Pour olive oil in slow cooker.

2. Layer the eggplant, squash, zucchini, onion and bell pepper in slow cooker.

3. Pour marinara sauce over the vegetables.

4. Cover slow cooker with lid and cook on low for 7 hours.

5. Garnish with basil and cheese. Serve hot with rice (optional) and enjoy.

Nutritional Information per Serving:

Calories 372

Fat 11 g

Saturated Fat 8.7 g

Carbohydrates 32.8 g

Protein 14.6 g

Sweet and Spicy Mixed Nuts

Serves: 4 - 6

Ingredients:

1 cup walnut

1 cup almonds

1 cup cashew

1 cup pecans

4 tablespoon honey

1/4 teaspoon cayenne pepper

2 teaspoon salt

Directions:

1. Spray inside of cooker with non stick spray. Add ingredients & mix well.

2. Cover slow cooker with lid and cook on high for 30 minutes.

3. Uncover the slow cooker and reduce the heat to low and cook for 2 hours. Stir occasionally.

4. Cool the nuts completely then serve.

Nutritional Information per Serving:

Calories 355

Fat 28 g

Saturated Fat 6.2 g

Carbohydrates 15.4 g

Sugar 7.5 g

Protein 9.2 g

Vegetable Rice

Serves: 2 - 3

Ingredients:

1 tablespoon olive oil

2 tablespoon brown sugar

2 celery ribs, chopped

1 tomato, sliced

1 green bell pepper, cut into strips

1 small white onion, sliced

1/2 tablespoon dried basil

8 ounce zucchini, sliced

8 ounce yellow squash, sliced

1/4 cup long grain rice, uncooked

Pepper

Salt

½ cup water

Directions:

1. Spread rice in slow cooker, with water. Then layer onion, squash, zucchini and basil.

2. Cover top with sliced tomatoes, celery and green pepper.

3. Sprinkle pepper, brown sugar and salt over the top of vegetable.

4. Drizzle with olive oil.

5. Cover the slow cooker with lid and cook on high for 4 hours.

6. Serve hot and enjoy.

Nutritional Information per Serving:

Calories 177

Fat 6 g

Saturated Fat 0.6 g

Carbohydrates 25 g

Protein 5 g

Quinoa and Kale Soup

Serves: 3 - 4

Ingredients:

2 cups vegetable stock

1 bay leave

1/2 cup quinoa, uncooked and rinsed

8 ounce canned black beans, rinsed and drained

3 tomatoes, diced

ounce kale, chopped

1/8 teaspoon dried thyme

1/4 teaspoon dried basil

1/8 teaspoon dried rosemary

1/4 teaspoon oregano

1 garlic clove, minced

1 medium white onion, diced

1 cup water

Pepper

Salt

Directions:

1. Combine onion, garlic, bay leave, quinoa, oregano, rosemary, basil, thyme, tomatoes and beans in slow cooker.

2. Pour vegetable stock and water in cooker.

3. Season with pepper and salt.

4. Cover slow cooker with lid and cook on low for 7 hours. Stir in kale.

5. Serve immediately and enjoy.

Nutritional Information per Serving:

- Calories 164
- Fat 2 g
- Saturated Fat 0 g
- Carbohydrates 30 g
- Protein 8 g

Lentil Chili

Serves: 2 - 4

Ingredients:

1/4 cup quinoa, uncooked

1/2 cup dried lentils

8 ounce canned kidney beans

1/2 tablespoon oregano

1 teaspoon cumin

1 tablespoon chili powder

1 cup water

2 cups vegetable stock

8 ounce canned tomatoes, diced

1 bell pepper, chopped

1/2 celery stalk, chopped

1 garlic clove, minced

1 small onion, chopped

Shredded cheese

Directions:

1. Combine all ingredients in slow cooker.

2. Cover slow cooker with lid and cook on low for 8 hours. Stir well before serving.

3. Serve chili with shredded cheese and enjoy.

Nutritional Information per Serving:

Calories 178

Fat 2 g

Saturated Fat 0 g

Carbohydrates 32 g

Protein 10 g

Corn and Potato Soup

Serves: 2 - 4

Ingredients:

2 cups vegetable stock

1/4 teaspoon ground coriander

1/4 teaspoon oregano

1/2 teaspoon cumin

1 jalapeno, sliced

1 can corn, drained

3 cups red potatoes, cut into chunks

1/4 teaspoon salt

Chives

Directions:

1. Combine vegetable stock, coriander, oregano, cumin, salt, jalapeno, corn and potatoes in slow cooker.

2. Cook on low for 7 hours. Stir before serving.

3. Pour the soup in serving bowls and garnish with chives.

4. Serve hot and enjoy.

Nutritional Information per Serving:

Calories 122

Fat 1 g

Saturated Fat 0 g

Carbohydrates 25 g

Protein 3 g

Cheesy Garlic Risotto

Serves: 2 - 4

Ingredients:

3/4 cup parmesan cheese, shredded

1 cup Arborio rice, uncooked

1 tablespoon onion flakes, dried

4 cups vegetable stock

1 tablespoon garlic powder

4 tablespoon olive oil

1/2 teaspoon black pepper

1 teaspoon salt

Freshly chopped chives

Directions:

1. Combine Arborio rice, garlic powder, onion flakes, black pepper and salt in slow cooker.

2. Add vegetable stock and olive oil in cooker. Stir once.

3. Cover and cook on high for 2 hours.

4. Uncover slow cooker and add cheese. Stir well until combine.

5. Garnish with chives and serve.

Nutritional Information per Serving:

Calories 303

Fat 14 g

Saturated Fat 2.1 g

Carbohydrates 40 g

Protein 5g

Apricot Rice

Serves: 2 - 4

Ingredients:

1/4 cup dried apricots, chopped

1/4 cup dried cranberries

1/4 cup almonds, sliced

2 cups vegetable stock

1 celery stalks, chopped

1 small onion, chopped

1 cup wild rice

1 tsp coconut oil

Directions:

1. Add wild rice in slow cooker.

2. Sauté onion and celery, in sauce pan, in light coconut oil.

3. Season with pepper and salt. Transfer onion mixture in slow cooker.

4. Add apricots and cranberries in cooker.

5. Cover slow cooker with lid and cook on low for 7 hours.

6. Uncover slow cooker and add almonds stir well and serve.

Nutritional Information per Serving:

Calories 330

Fat 15 g

Saturated Fat 7g

Carbohydrates 35g

Protein 8 g

Lentil and Chickpea Curry

Serves: 3 - 6

Ingredients:

30 ounce canned chickpeas, drained

15 ounce canned coconut milk

1 cup red lentils, rinsed

1 medium onion, chopped

2 cups vegetable stock

2 garlic cloves, minced

1 cup pumpkin puree

1/4 teaspoon ground cayenne pepper

1 tablespoon curry powder

1 teaspoon salt

Freshly Chopped cilantro

Directions:

1. Add all ingredients in slow cooker except coconut milk.

2. Cover slow cooker with lid and cook on low for 7 hours.

3. Uncover slow cooker and add coconut milk stir well and cook another 30 minutes.

4. Garnish with chopped cilantro and serve with steam rice.

Nutritional Information per Serving:

Calories 400

Fat 8 g

Carbohydrates 50 g

Protein 25 g

Spicy Potato Fries

Serves: 2 - 4

Ingredients:

- 4 cups Russet potatoes, diced
- 1 teaspoon chili powder
- 1 teaspoon paprika
- 2 tablespoon olive oil
- 1 teaspoon black pepper
- 1 teaspoon salt

Directions:

1. Heat olive oil in cooker over the medium heat and add potatoes and sauté for 4 minutes.

2. Then add chili powder, paprika, pepper and salt. Stir well.

3. Cover the slow cooker with lid and cook on high for 7 minutes.

4. Turn off the heat and release the pressure using quick release method.

5. Serve hot fries with sauce and enjoy.

Nutritional Information per Serving:

Calories 188

Fat 7 g

Saturated Fat 1.1 g

Carbohydrates 24 g

Protein 2 g

Slow Cooker Carrots

Serves: 2 - 5

Ingredients:

16 ounce carrots, peeled and cut into

1/2 inch wedges

1 bay leaves

1 tblsp brown sugar

1/8 cup melted butter, salted

1/2 teaspoon vanilla extract

Freshly chopped parsley

1/4 teaspoon salt

Directions:

1. Add all ingredients in slow cooker except parsley and mix well until combined.

2. Cover slow cooker with lid and cook on high for 3 hours or until carrots are tender.

3. Garnish carrots with parsley and serve.

Nutritional Information per Serving:

Calories 93

Fat 4 g

Carbohydrates 12 g

Protein 1 g

Mashed Potatoes

Serves: 2 - 4

Ingredients:

4 large russet potatoes, peeled and cubed

1/8 cup fresh chives, chopped

1/2 cup sour cream

1/4 cup parmesan cheese, grated

Directions:

1. In a large pot, add potatoes and pinch of salt.

2. Pour cold water in pot and bring to boil. Reduce heat and simmer for 25 minutes.

3. Drain potatoes and add them in electric mixer. Then add sour cream, & half cheese.

4. Season with pepper and salt. Beat until get smooth and light mixture.

5. Add potato mixture, remaining cheese into the slow cooker and cook on low for 4 hours.

6. Serve warm and enjoy.

Nutritional Information per Serving:

Calories 466

Fat 22 g

Saturated Fat 13 g

Carbohydrates 60 g

Protein 9 g

Slow cooker Black Beans

Serves: 2 - 4

Ingredients:

2 1/2 cups vegetable stock

8 ounce black beans, overnight soaked
and drained

1 bay leaf

1 tablespoon lime juice

8 ounce canned tomatoes, crushed

1/2 teaspoon spice mix seasoning

1 small red pepper, chopped

1 medium white onion, chopped

1 tablespoon olive oil

1 garlic clove, chopped

Directions:

1. Add soaked black beans in slow cooker.

2. In a pan, heat olive oil over the medium heat and add garlic, onion, red pepper and seasoning sauté until onion becomes soften.

3. Cover slow cooker with lid and cook on high for 5 hours.

4. Serve beans with tacos and enjoy.

Nutritional Information per Serving:

Calories 251

Fat 5 g

Saturated Fat 0.7 g

Carbohydrates 41 g

Protein 13 g

Squash, Corn and Tomatoes

Serves: 3 - 6

Ingredients:

4 yellow squash, diced

6 cups frozen sweet corn kernels

2 cups cherry tomatoes

2 tbsp coconut oil

Pepper

Salt

Directions:

1. Add squash, corn, tomatoes and oil in slow cooker mix well until combine.

2. Season with pepper and salt.

3. Cover the slow cooker with lid and cook on high for 2 hours.

4. Serve hot and enjoy.

Nutritional Information per Serving:

Calories 292

Fat 16g

Saturated Fat 9.5 g

Carbohydrates 36 g

Protein 6 g

Glazed Baby Carrots

Serves: 6 - 8

Ingredients:

4 pounds baby carrots

1 cup vegetable stock

2 teaspoon dried thyme

2 cup orange juice

1/2 cup honey

½ cup butter

Pepper

Salt

Directions:

1. Add carrots, thyme, honey, butter, orange juice and vegetable stock in slow cooker mix well until combine.

2. Season with pepper and salt.

3. Cover the slow cooker with lid and cook on low for 5 hours.

4. Serve warm and enjoy.

Nutritional Information per Serving:

Calories 221

Fat 4 g

Carbohydrates 40 g

Protein 5 g

Sweet Potato Soup

Serves: 3 - 4

Ingredients:

1/2 cup slice almonds

1 cinnamon stick

1 tablespoon curry powder

1 tablespoon fresh ginger, grated

2 pound sweet potatoes

2 medium carrot

2 white onion

Pepper

Salt

Directions:

1. Combine all ingredients in slow cooker except almonds.

2. Cover slow cooker with lid and cook on low for 5 hours.

3. Using immersion blender blend soup until get smooth puree.

4. Garnish soup with sliced almonds.

5. Serve hat and enjoy.

Nutritional Information per Serving:

Calories 312

Fat 4 g

Carbohydrates 63 g   Protein 5g

Slow Cooker Chickpea Soup

Serves: 3 - 4

Ingredients:

15 ounce canned chickpeas, drained and

rinsed

1/2 red onion, chopped

1 garlic clove, minced

2 cups vegetable stock

1/8 fresh parsley, chopped

1/2 tablespoon olive oil

1 tablespoon lemon juice

1/4 teaspoon cumin

1/2 teaspoon salt

Directions:

1. Add chickpeas, onion, garlic, vegetable stock, cumin and salt in slow cooker mix well and cook on low for 4 hours.

2. Allow to cool soup slightly then using blender blends the soup.

3. Place soup again in slow cooker then add parsley, olive oil and lemon juice mix well. Cook on low for another 30 minutes.

4. Serve hot and enjoy.

Nutritional Information per Serving:

Calories 180

Fat 2g

Carbohydrates 30 g   Protein 13 g

Stuffed Tomatoes

Serves: 4 - 6

Ingredients:

6 large tomatoes, halved

4 cups breadcrumbs

1/4 cup olive oil

1/2 cup fresh basil, chopped

1/2 cup fresh parsley, chopped

4 garlic cloves, minced

1 cup parmesan cheese, grated

1 cup Romano cheese, grated

Pepper

Salt

Directions:

1. In a bowl, combine together breadcrumbs, basil, parsley, garlic, parmesan cheese and Romano cheese.

2. Pour olive oil in slow cooker. Stuffed cheese mixture into the halved tomatoes and place in slow cooker.

3. Season stuffed tomatoes with pepper and salt.

4. Cover slow cooker with lid and cook on low for 4 hours.

5. Serve warm and enjoy.

Nutritional Information per Serving:

Calories 197

Fat 6 g   Carbohydrates 30 g   Protein 6 g

Sweet Potato Red Lentil

Serves: 3 - 6

Ingredients:

2 large sweet potatoes, diced

2 cups vegetable stocks

1 cup water

1 white onion, chopped

1 can coconut milk

1 cup red lentil, uncooked

2 teaspoon ground coriander

2 teaspoon chili powder

3 garlic cloves, minced

1/2 teaspoon salt

Directions:

1. Add sweet potatoes, ground coriander, garlic, chili powder, onion and vegetable stock in slow cooker mix well and cook on high for 3 hours.

2. Uncover slow cooker and add lentil stir well cover cooker again and cook on high for another 1 hour.

3. Stir coconut milk and water to get desire consistency.

4. Serve warm and enjoy.

Nutritional Information per Serving:

Calories 125

Fat 1g

Carbohydrates 21g   Protein 8g

We hope that you enjoy these recipes for years to come, with your families, and friends! We appreciate your reviews so much, and thank you for cooking with us! Be sure to join us on Facebook, Instagram, & our mailing list. For so much more! Find links inside the FREE preview of this books eBook version on Amazon.

Anti – Inflammatory Diet

Slow Cooker

Anti – Inflammation Diet Recipes

Cindy Myers

Recipe Junkies

Slow Cooker Chicken

Serves: 4 - 6

Preparation Time: 6 hours 10 minutes

Ingredients:

- 2.5 pound chicken, skinless
- 1/4 cup lemon juice
- 1/2 teaspoon dried rosemary
- 1/2 tablespoon oregano
- 1 teaspoon whole cloves
- 1/4 teaspoon black pepper
- 1/2 white onion, chopped

- 1/8 teaspoon black pepper
- 2 carrots, cubed
- 4 medium golden potatoes, quartered
- 2 teaspoon garlic salt

Directions:

1. Combine together sliced onions, carrots, potatoes, 1/2 teaspoon garlic salt and 1/8 teaspoon black pepper into the slow cooker.

2. In a mixing bowl, add chicken, chopped onion, garlic salt, whole cloves and black pepper mix well until evenly coated.

3. Then place chicken in slow cooker.

4. Sprinkle oregano and rosemary over the chicken.

5. Then pour lemon juice over the chicken.

6. Cover slow cooker with lid and cook on low for 6 hours.

Nutritional Value (Amount per Serving):

- Calories 300
- Fat 5 g
- Carbohydrates 30g
- Protein 30 g

Tropic Chicken

Serves: 4 - 6

Preparation Time: 6 hours 10 minutes

Ingredients:

- 1.5 pound chicken breast, halved, boneless and skinless
- 1/8 teaspoon ground ginger
- 1/8 teaspoon salt
- 1 tablespoon lemon juice
- 1 tablespoon brown sugar
- 1 tablespoon cornstarch
- 8 ounce can oranges, drained
- 8 ounce can pineapple slices, drained

Directions:

1. Place chicken breast in slow cooker.

2. In a mixing bowl mix together remaining ingredients and spread over the chicken evenly.

3. Cover slow cooker with lid and cook on low for 6 hours.

Nutritional Value (Amount per Serving):

- Calories 200
- Fat 6 g
- Carbohydrates 4 g
- Protein 30 g

Slow Cooker Cheese Soufflé

Serves: 2 - 4

Preparation Time: 3 hours 5 minutes

Ingredients:

- 2 eggs
- 1 cups fat free coconut milk (plain)
- 1/8 teaspoon cayenne
- 4 ounce shredded cheddar cheese
- 4 bread slices (whole grain)

- 4 ounce shredded mozzarella cheese (optional)

Directions:

1. Mix together cheese and set aside.
2. Tear the bread slices into the pieces and set aside.
3. Spray the slow cooker with non-stick cooking spray.
4. Layer the bread and cheese alternately in slow cooker.
5. In a bowl, whisk together eggs, milk and cayenne. Pour the egg mixture over the bread and cheese layers.

6. Cover the slow cooker with lid and cook on low for 3 hours.

7. Serve warm and enjoy.

Nutritional Value (Amount per Serving):

- Calories 238
- Fat 12 g
- Carbohydrates 17g
- Protein 13g

Stuffed Peppers

Serves: 4 - 8

Preparation Time: 6 hours 10 minutes

Ingredients:

- 8 bell peppers, remove seeds and cap
- 2 cups cooked jasmine rice
- 1 cup water
- 1/2 cup diced white onion
- 2 cups broccoli florets
- 2 canned tomatoes, diced
- 1/2 teaspoon black pepper
- 1/2 teaspoon chili powder
- 1 teaspoon ground chipotle
- 1/4 teaspoon salt

Directions:

1. Place bell peppers in slow cooker.

2. In a mixing bowl, mix together rice, onions, broccoli, tomatoes and mix spices.

3. Spoon the mixture into the each bell pepper and replace the cap.

4. Pour the water into the bottom of slow cooker.

5. Cover slow cooker with lid and cook on slow for 6 hours.

Nutritional Value (Amount per Serving):

- Calories 150
- Fat 1 g
- Carbohydrates 30 g
- Protein 5 g

Zucchini Stew

Serves: 3 - 4

Preparation Time: 4 hours 10 minutes

Ingredients:

- 3/4 cup sweet corn kernels
- 3 tablespoon lemon juice
- 1 tablespoon fresh dill, minced
- 3 cups zucchini, sliced
- 1 red onion, sliced
- 1/4 teaspoon black pepper
- 1/4 teaspoon salt

Directions:

1. Add all ingredients in slow cooker except corn. Mix well.

2. Cover slow cooker with lid and cook on low for 3 hours.

3. Uncover the cooker and stir corn. Cook again on low for 1 hour.

4. Serve hot and enjoy.

Nutritional Value (Amount per Serving):

- Calories 45
- Fat 1 g
- Carbohydrates 8 g
- Protein 1g

Cheesy Corn

Serves: 3 - 5

Preparation Time: 4 hours 10 minutes

Ingredients:

- 24 ounce frozen corn
- 2 tablespoon almond milk (vanilla)
- 2 tablespoon water
- 2 tablespoon coconut oil
- 3 cheese slices, cut into squares
- 4 ounce cream cheese, cubed

Directions:

1. Add corn, milk, water, oil, slice cheese and cream cheese mix well until combined.

2. Cover the slow cooker with lid and cook on low for 4 hours.

Nutritional Value (Amount per Serving):

- Calories 309
- Fat 15g
- Carbohydrates 20g
- Protein 9 g

Slow Cooker Franks

Serves: 2 - 4

Preparation Time: 7 hours 10 minutes

Ingredients:

- 1 pound mini cocktail franks
- 1/4 teaspoon ground ginger
- 1 tablespoon soy sauce
- 1/4 cup vegetable stock
- 1 garlic clove, minced
- 1/2 white onion, chopped
- 1 tablespoon apple cider vinegar
- 3 tablespoon tomato sauce

- 3 tablespoon apricot preserves
- Pinch of white pepper

Directions:

1. Add all ingredients in slow cooker except franks mix well until combine.

2. Now stir in franks.

3. Cover slow cooker with lid and cook on low for 7 hours.

Nutritional Value (Amount per Serving):

- Calories 130
- Fat 5 g
- Carbohydrates 12 g
- Protein 6g

Sweet Potato Casserole

Serves: 2 - 4

Preparation Time: 6 hours 10 minutes

Ingredients:

- 1 tablespoon coconut flour
- 1/4 cup cashew milk
- 1 egg, beaten
- 3 tablespoon pecans, chopped
- 1/2 tablespoon orange juice
- 1 tablespoon brown sugar
- 2 teaspoon coconut oil

- 15 ounce can sweet potatoes, drained

Directions:

1. Spray slow cooker with non-stick cooking spray.
2. Mash the sweet potatoes with 1 teaspoon oil, sugar, brown sugar, eggs, milk and orange juice.
3. Transfer sweet potatoes mixture into the slow cooker.
4. Add remaining oil, flour and pecans in bowl use fork to blend.
5. Sprinkle pecans mixture over the sweet potatoes.

6. Cover the slow cooker with lid and cook on low for 6 hours.

Nutritional Value (Amount per Serving):

- Calories 90
- Fat 3 g
- Carbohydrates 10 g
- Protein 4g

Stewed Okra

Serves: 4 - 8

Preparation Time: 2 hours 10 minutes

Ingredients:

- 2 teaspoon hot sauce

- 4 garlic cloves, minced

- 1 medium sweet onion, diced

- 3 cups okra, diced

- 4 tomatoes, diced

Directions:

1. Place tomatoes, okra, onion, garlic and hot sauce in slow cooker. Stir well.

2. Cook on low for 2 hours.

3. Stir once before serving.

Nutritional Value (Amount per Serving):

- Calories 48
- Fat 1 g
- Carbohydrates 7 g
- Protein 2 g

Pistachios Coconut Rice

Serves: 3 - 6

Preparation Time: 4 hours 10 minutes

Ingredients:

- 4 tablespoon pistachios, toasted and chopped
- 1/2 teaspoon turmeric
- 1/2 cup water
- 2 cups coconut milk
- 1 cup white rice, uncooked
- 1 lemon juice
- 1/2 teaspoon salt

Directions:

1. Add rice, coconut milk, lemon juice, turmeric, water and salt in slow cooker mix well until combine.

2. Cover slow cooker with lid and cook on low for 4 hours.

3. Stir pistachios before serving.

4. Serve warm and enjoy.

Nutritional Value (Amount per Serving):

- Calories 240
- Fat 9 g
- Carbohydrates 30 g
- Protein 7 g

Slow Cooker Chickpeas

Serves: 3 - 6

Preparation Time: 5 hours 5 minutes

Ingredients:

- 14 ounce can chickpeas, drained
- 1/2 teaspoon cumin powder
- 1 teaspoon curry powder
- 1/2 tablespoon lemon juice

Directions:

1. In a bowl, add cumin powder, lemon juice, chickpeas and curry powder mix well until combine.
2. Transfer chickpeas mixture into the slow cooker.
3. Cover the slow cooker with lid and cook on high for 5 hours.

Nutritional Value (Amount per Serving):

- Calories 82
- Fat 1 g
- Carbohydrates 15 g
- Protein 3 g

Pinto Bean Rice

Serves: 3 - 6

Preparation Time: 6 hours 10 minutes

Ingredients:

- 1 1/4 cups vegetable stock
- 1 cup wild rice
- 15 ounce can tomatoes, diced
- 1/2 tablespoon dried onion flakes
- 1 teaspoon Italian seasoning
- 15 ounce can pinto beans, drained
- 15 ounce can black beans, drained
- 1 tablespoon coconut oil
- 1/2 teaspoon salt

Directions:

1. Add olive oil in slow cooker over medium heat then add rice and sauté for 1 minute.

2. Now add remaining ingredients and mix well.

3. Cover slow cooker with lid and cook on low for 6 hours.

4. Serve hot and enjoy.

Nutritional Value (Amount per Serving):

- Calories 217
- Fat 3 g
- Carbohydrates 41 g
- Protein 6 g

Coconut Rice

Serves: 4 - 8

Preparation Time: 5 hours 5 minutes

Ingredients:

- 1/3 cup shredded coconut
- 1/4 cup sugar
- 3 cups low fat almond milk
- 3/4 cup white rice
- 1/4 teaspoon orange peel
- 1/2 teaspoon vanilla
- 1/4 teaspoon salt

Directions:

1. Add all ingredients in slow cooker cover and cook on low for 8 hours.

2. Serve hot and enjoy.

Nutritional Value (Amount per Serving):

- Calories 177
- Fat 2g
- Carbohydrates 35 g
- Protein 4 g

Searching for a great guide, on the subject? Look this informative guide up, on Amazon.

Black Bean Soup

Serves: 4 - 6

Preparation Time: 6 hours 5 minutes

Ingredients:

- 2 can black beans, drained
- 2 can vegetable stock
- 6 tablespoon hot thick salsa
- 2 tablespoon red wine (optional)

Directions:

1. Add beans, salsa, vegetable stock and wine in slow cooker.

2. Cover slow cooker with lid and cook on low for 6 hours.

3. Using hand blender, blend until get desire consistency. (optional)

4. Serve hot and enjoy.

Nutritional Value (Amount per Serving):

- Calories 100

- Fat 3 g

- Carbohydrates 13 g

- Protein 4 g

Noodles and Corn

Serves: 4 - 6

Preparation Time: 6 hours 10 minutes

Ingredients:

- 1 egg, beaten
- 2 cups sweet corn
- 3/4 cup shredded cheddar cheese
- 3 cups cooked penne noodles
- 2 tbsp cup coconut oil
- 1/2 teaspoon salt

Directions:

1. Combine all ingredients in slow cooker. Cover and cook on low for 6 hours.

2. Serve hot and enjoy.

Nutritional Value (Amount per Serving):

- Calories 255
- Fat 12 g
- Carbohydrates 30 g
- Protein 9g

Carrot Casserole

Serves: 4 - 6

Preparation Time: 4 hours 5 minutes

Ingredients:

- 1/2 cup vegan cheese
- 10 ounce can cream celery soup
- 1 medium sweet onion, chopped
- 4 cups carrots, sliced
- 1/2 teaspoon salt

Directions:

1. Mix all ingredients in slow cooker. Cover and cook on low for 4 hours or until carrots are tender.

2. Serve hot and enjoy.

Nutritional Value (Amount per Serving):

- Calories 113
- Fat 4 g
- Carbohydrates 13g
- Protein 4 g

Slow Oregano Tomatoes

Serves: 2 - 4

Preparation Time: 1 hour 5 minutes

Ingredients:

- 1/4 teaspoon parsley, chopped
- 1/4 teaspoon dried oregano
- 1/4 teaspoon dried basil
- 1/2 tablespoon olive oil
- 4 tomatoes, halved

Directions:

1. Spray slow cooker with non-stick cooking spray.

2. Place tomatoes in slow cooker and drizzle with olive oil.

3. Sprinkle oregano, basil and parsley over the tomatoes.

4. Cover slow cooker with lid and cook on high for 1 hour.

5. Serve warm and enjoy.

Nutritional Value (Amount per Serving):

- Calories 30
- Fat 1 g
- Carbohydrates 2 g
- Protein 1 g

Sour Zucchini

Serves: 4 - 6

Preparation Time: 1 hour 10 minutes

Ingredients:

- 1 cup shredded cheddar cheese
- 1 cup green onion, chopped
- 1/4 cup almond milk
- 1 cup sour cream
- 4 cups sliced zucchini
- 1 teaspoon salt

Directions:

1. Spray slow cooker with non-stick cooking spray.
2. Place zucchini in slow cooker.

3. In a small bowl, combine together onions, milk, sour cream and salt. Pour the mixture over zucchini and stir well.

4. Cover slow cooker with lid and cook on low for 1 hour.

5. Sprinkle cheddar cheese over the zucchini before 15 minutes of serving.

6. Serve warm and enjoy.

Nutritional Value (Amount per Serving):

- Calories 183
- Fat 14g
- Carbohydrates 6g
- Protein 7g

Slow Cooker Apples and Squash

Serves: 4 - 6

Preparation Time: 6 hours 15 minutes

Ingredients:

- 2 honey crisp apples, cored and slices
- 1 butternut squash, seeded cut into slices
- 1/4 cup apple juice
- Pinch of cinnamon
- 3 tablespoon raisins

Directions:

1. Layer half ingredients in slow cooker apples, squash and raisins.
2. Repeat layers then pour apple juice over the top.
3. Cook on low for 6 hours.

Nutritional Value (Amount per Serving):

- Calories 69
- Fat 1g
- Carbohydrates 17g
- Protein 1 g

Green Beans

Serves: 4 - 6

Preparation Time: 5 hours 10 minutes

Ingredients:

- 1 cup vegan cheese
- 1/2 cup white onion, chopped
- 1/2 cup almond milk
- 1 tablespoon coconut flour
- 16 ounce can green beans, drained

Directions:

1. Place onions, cheese and green beans in slow cooker. Stir well together.
2. In a bowl, combine together milk and flour.

3. Pour the milk and flour mixture over the beans.

4. Cover the slow cooker with lid and cook on low for 5 hours.

Nutritional Value (Amount per Serving):

- Calories 118
- Fat 6 g
- Carbohydrates 8 g
- Protein 7 g

Potato Salad

Serves: 4 - 8

Preparation Time: 6 hours 15 minutes

Ingredients:

- 1/4 cup fresh parsley
- 2 tablespoon quick cooking tapioca
- 1/3 cup vinegar
- 1 cup water
- 1 cup celery, chopped
- 1 cup red onion, chopped
- 1/4 teaspoon black pepper
- 6 golden potatoes, sliced
- 1 teaspoon salt

Directions:

1. Combine onions, celery and potatoes in slow cooker.

2. In a small bowl, combine vinegar, tapioca, salt, water, and black pepper.

3. Pour the mixture over the top of potatoes and mix gently.

4. Cover and cook on low for 6 hours.

Nutritional Value (Amount per Serving):

- Calories 112
- Fat 1 g
- Carbohydrates 25g
- Protein 2g

Sweet Potatoes Applesauce

Serves: 3 - 6

Preparation Time: 6 hours 15 minutes

Ingredients:

- 6 medium sweet potatoes, peeled and sliced
- 1 teaspoon cinnamon
- 1 tablespoon coconut oil (optional)
- 1/3 cup brown sugar (optional)
- 1 1/2 cups applesauce
- Chopped nuts

Directions:

1. Add sliced sweet potatoes in slow cooker.

2. In a bowl, mix together cinnamon, oil, brown sugar and applesauce. Pour the mixture over the top of potatoes.

3. Cover and cook on low for 6 hours.

4. Mash potatoes slightly and add chopped nuts.

5. Serve warm and enjoy.

Nutritional Value (Amount per Serving):

- Calories 140
- Fat 5 g
- Carbohydrates 23g
- Protein 1 g

Spicy Cashews

Serves: 2 - 4

Preparation Time: 2 hours 10 minutes

Ingredients:

- 4 cups cashews
- 1/4 teaspoon ground all spice
- 1/4 teaspoon sweet paprika
- 1 teaspoon ground cinnamon
- 1/4 teaspoon cayenne pepper
- 1 teaspoon ground coriander
- 1 teaspoon ground cumin
- 1/4 teaspoon ground ginger
- 1/4 cup maple syrup
- 1/2 teaspoon salt

Directions:

1. Spray slow cooker with non-stick cooking spray.

2. In small bowl, mix together all ingredients except cashew.

3. Place cashew in slow cooker.

4. Pour the spice mixture over the cashew and mix well until evenly coated.

5. Cook on low for 2 hours stir occasionally.

6. Allow to cool completely then serve.

Nutritional Value (Amount per Serving):

- Calories 380
- Fat 20g
- Carbohydrates 28 g
- Protein 12g

Pumpkin Quinoa

Serves: 4 - 6

Preparation Time: 6 hours 10 minutes

Ingredients:

- 1/2 cup can pumpkin
- 4 cup almond milk, unsweetened
- 1 cup quinoa, rinsed and drained
- 1/4 teaspoon ground all spice
- 1 teaspoon ground cinnamon
- 1/4 teaspoon nutmeg
- 1 teaspoon vanilla extract
- 1/4 teaspoon ground ginger
- 1/4 cup maple syrup
- 1/2 teaspoon salt
- Toasted pecans, chopped

Directions:

1. Place all ingredients in slow cooker except pecans mix well until combined.

2. Cover and cook on low for 6 hours.

3. Garnish with toasted pecans and serve hot.

Nutritional Value (Amount per Serving):

- Calories 195
- Fat 3 g
- Carbohydrates 25 g
- Protein 12 g

Slow Cooker Herb Beets

Serves: 2 - 4

Preparation Time: 6 hours 5 minutes

Ingredients:

- 2 teaspoon dried thyme

- 1 teaspoon crushed mint leaves

- 1/2 cup water

- 4 beets, peeled and diced

- Salt

Directions:

1. Combine thyme, mint leaves, water and beets together in slow cooker.

2. Season with salt and cook on low for 6 hours.

3. Remove thyme springs and store in airtight container.

Nutritional Value (Amount per Serving):

- Calories 49
- Fat 0 g
- Carbohydrates 10g
- Protein 2g

Roasted Veggies

Serves: 4 - 6

Preparation Time: 4 hours 10 minutes

Ingredients:

- 8 baby carrots
- 8 Brussels sprouts
- 4 tablespoon chicken bouillon (optional)
- 8 pearl onions
- 1 teaspoon rubbed sage
- 1 teaspoon dried rosemary
- 2 teaspoon dried thyme
- 2 tablespoon olive oil
- 1/4 cup water
- Pepper

- Salt

Directions:

1. Add olive oil in slow cooker over the medium heat then add all ingredients in slow cooker. Mix well.

2. Cook on low for 4 hours.

3. Season with pepper and salt to taste.

Nutritional Value (Amount per Serving):

- Calories 156
- Fat 4 g
- Carbohydrates 26 g
- Protein 4 g

Pineapple Yams

Serves: 3 - 5

Preparation Time: 2 hours 5 minutes

Ingredients:

- 20 ounce can unsweetened yams, drained
- 5 ounce can unsweetened crushed pineapple, drained

Directions:

1. Place yams in slow cooker and pour pineapple over the top. Mix well.

2. Cover and cook on low for 2 hours.

Nutritional Value (Amount per Serving):

- Calories 155
- Fat 0.2 g
- Carbohydrates 37g
- Protein 2g

Slow Cooker Herbed Rice

Serves: 3 - 6

Preparation Time: 4 hours 5 minutes

Ingredients:

- 1 cup long grain rice, uncooked
- 3 cups water
- 3 chicken bouillon cubes
- 1/2 cup almonds
- 1/4 cup onions, diced
- 1/4 cup dried parsley, chopped
- 1/2 teaspoon dried marjoram

- 1 teaspoon dried rosemary

Directions:

1. Mix together water and chicken bouillon cubes.
2. Combine all ingredients in slow cooker and pour water and bouillon cubes in cooker.
3. Cook on low for 4 hours.

Nutritional Value (Amount per Serving):

- Calories 183
- Fat 6.g
- Carbohydrates 27 g
- Protein 4 g

Rice and Red Beans Stew

Serves: 3 - 6

Preparation Time: 6 hours 15 minutes

Ingredients:

- 6 carrots, peeled and sliced

- 3/4 cup brown rice, uncooked

- 2 cups dried red beans, soaked overnight

- 4 cups water

- 1 tablespoon cumin

- 1 large onion, chopped

- 1 teaspoon salt

Directions:

1. Drained red beans and place in slow cooker then stir remaining ingredients.

2. Cover and cook on low for 6 hours.

3. Serve hot and enjoy.

Nutritional Value (Amount per Serving):

- Calories 231
- Fat 1.5 g
- Carbohydrates 40 g
- Protein 16g

Black-Eyed Pea Dip

Serves: 3 - 6

Preparation Time: 2 hours 10 minutes

Ingredients:

- 8 ounce can black-eyed peas, drained
- 4 ounce vegan cheese, cubed
- 2 chopped green onions
- 2 ounce can green chilies

Directions:

1. Add black-eyed peas, cheese, onions, and green chilies in slow cooker.

2. Cover and cook on low for 2 hours.

3. Serve warm with tortilla chips and enjoy.

Nutritional Value (Amount per Serving):

- Calories 176
- Fat 14 g
- Carbohydrates 6 g
- Protein 6 g

Egg Casserole

Serves: 3 - 6

Preparation Time: 6 hours 10 minutes

Ingredients:

- 6 - 12 slice whole grain sandwich bread
- 2 ounce fat free ham slice, diced
- 4 ounce can green chilies, drained
- 1/3 cup shredded cheddar cheese
- 1/4 teaspoon paprika
- 1/2 teaspoon black pepper
- 6 eggs, beaten

- Salt

Directions:

1. In a mixing bowl, mix all ingredients together except bread slices.

2. Place bread on bottom of slow cooker.

3. Pour egg mixture over the bread.

4. Cook on low for 6 hours.

Nutritional Value (Amount per Serving):

- Calories 207
- Fat 10g
- Carbohydrates 13 g
- Protein 11 g

Mashed Potato with Garlic

Serves: 3 - 5

Preparation Time: 3 hours 5 minutes

Ingredients:

- 1.5 pound golden potatoes, peeled and quartered
- 1/4 cup sour cream
- 2 tablespoon cashew milk
- 1/2 tablespoon parsley, minced
- 1/4 cup vegetable stock
- 2 garlic cloves, minced
- Pepper
- Salt

Directions:

1. Place potatoes, vegetable stock and parsley in slow cooker stir well.

2. Cover and cook on high for 3 hours.

3. Pour sour cream and milk.

4. Using masher mash the potatoes.

5. Season with pepper and salt.

6. Serve hot and enjoy.

Nutritional Value (Amount per Serving):

- Calories 134
- Fat 3 g
- Carbohydrates 22 g
- Protein 3 g

Slow Cooker Mac

Serves: 6 - 12

Preparation Time: 2 hours 5 minutes

Ingredients:

- 16 ounce macaroni, cooked
- 2 cups shredded cheddar cheese
- 4 cups low fat almond milk
- 1/2 teaspoon ground black pepper
- 1 tablespoon cornstarch
- 2 teaspoon dry mustard

Directions:

1. In a pan, heat cornstarch, milk, pepper and mustard until warm whisk occasionally then stir in the cheese.

2. Place macaroni into the slow cooker.

3. Pour milk and cheese mixture over the macaroni.

4. Cover and cook on low for 2 hours.

5. Serve hot and enjoy.

Nutritional Value (Amount per Serving):

- Calories 263
- Fat 7g
- Carbohydrates 35 g
- Protein 12.5 g

We thank you for ordering this book, and appreciate all of your reviews! Thank you. We hope you can enjoy these recipes, for years to come.

Here are some more slow cooker recipes, that you might enjoy!

Lemon Potatoes

Serves: 3 - 6

Preparation Time: 3 hours 15 minutes

Ingredients:

2 pound small potatoes

3 tablespoon fresh chives, snipped

1 tablespoon lemon juice

2 tablespoon melted butter

1/4 cup water

1/2 teaspoon black pepper

1 teaspoon salt

Fresh parsley, chopped

Directions:

Make a cut of strip around the middle of each potato.

Place potatoes in slow cooker and pour water over.

Cover slow cooker with lid and cook on high for 3 hours.

Drain potatoes completely.

Combine chives, lemon juice, butter and parsley.

Pour the butter mixture over the potatoes and toss well until coated.

Season with pepper and salt. Serve immediately and enjoy.

Nutritional Value (Amount per Serving):

Calories 120

Fat 3.8 g

Saturated Fat 2.1 g

Carbohydrates 21 g

Protein 3 g

Kidney and Black Beans Chili

Serves: 4 - 6

Preparation Time: 7 hours 20 minutes

Ingredients:

15 ounces canned kidney beans, rinsed and drained

1 cup corn kernels

15 ounces canned black beans, rinsed and drained

1 teaspoon cumin

2 teaspoon jalapeno hot sauce

1 teaspoon paprika

1 teaspoon chili powder

1 teaspoon cayenne

3 garlic cloves, minced

1 onion, chopped

2 carrots, diced

2 celery stalks, diced

25 ounces canned tomatoes, diced

1 teaspoon jalapeno, minced

Directions:

Add all ingredients in slow cooker

except corn.

Cover cooker with lid and cook on low for 6 hours.

Stir well and add corn kernels.

Cover the cooker again and cook on low for 1 hour.

Serve hot and enjoy.

Nutritional Value (Amount per Serving):

Calories 540 Fat 2.5 g

Carbohydrates 98 g Protein 33 g

White Bean Soup

Serves: 2 - 4

Preparation Time: 6 hours 5 minutes

Ingredients:

14 ounce canned white beans, rinsed and drained

3 cups vegetable stock

14 ounce canned tomatoes crushed, drained

1 onion, diced

1 carrot, diced

2 celery stalks, diced

1 garlic cloves, minced

2 tablespoon olive oil

Pepper

Salt

Directions:

In small pan, heat olive oil over medium heat and add onion, carrot, garlic and celery sauté until vegetables are soften.

Now add tomatoes in pan and combine well.

Transfer vegetable mixture into the slow cooker.

Add white beans and vegetable stock in cooker.

Close cooker with lid and cook on low for 6 hours.

Season with pepper and salt and serve hot.

Nutritional Value (Amount per Serving):

Calories 410

Fat 7.9 g

Saturated Fat 1.2 g

Carbohydrates 64 g Protein 23 g

Turkey stew with green chilies

Ingredients:

1 ½ cups butternut squash (peeled and diced)
1 lb. ground turkey
2 large potatoes (peeled and diced)
3 medium carrots (peeled and chopped)
1 onion (diced)
4 cloves garlic (minced)
1 tsp cumin
1 tsp chili powder
1 cup roasted chopped green chili
1 quart chicken stock
Low salt and black pepper to taste

For serving:

Juice from 1 lime
2-3 tbsp chopped cilantro
1-2 tsp agave nectar, as needed

Method:

1. Firstly, brown the ground pork in a skillet and take out the excess fat, if any.

2. Now add the pork to the slow cooker with the remaining ingredients up to sea salt and black pepper. Stir well to combine.

3. Cover and cook until the pork is done.

4. About 20 minutes before serving, stir in the lime juice and cilantro. Add some sweetener, if needed, to balance out the spice and if you need a little more liquid, add more broth to it and heat through.

Nutritional information:

Calories: 423 kcal; Fats: 13.5g; Carbohydrates: 44.7g; Protein: 36.3g

Crock Beans

Ingredients:

1 onion, chopped

3 cups of pinto beans

¼ cup of chopped jalapeno pepper

2 tablespoons of minced garlic

5 teaspoons of salt

¾ teaspoons of pepper

1/8 teaspoon of cumin

9 cups of water

Method:

1. Chop up the onion and place in the slow cooker with everything else

2. Cook on high for about five hours

3. Once the beans are cooked, strain them and mash them

4. Serve and enjoy

Nutritional Information;

Calories: 139 kcal, Fats: 0.5 grams, Carbohydrates: 25.4 grams, Protein: 8.5 grams

Vegetable and Cheese Soup

Ingredients:

3 cups of creamed corn

1 cup of potatoes, peeled and cubed

1 cup of carrots, chopped

½ onion, chopped

1 teaspoon of celery seed

½ teaspoon of pepper

6 cups of vegetable broth

3 cups of cheese sauce

Method:

1. Peel and chop everything then place in the slow cooker
2. Stir well and cook on medium heat for about five hours
3. Serve and enjoy

Nutritional Information:

Calories: 316 kcal, Fats: 16.5 grams, Carbohydrates: 32.1 grams, Protein: 11.9 grams

Vegetable and Black Bean Soup

Ingredients:

1 pound of black beans

1 ½ quarts of water

1 carrot, chopped

1 stalk of celery, chopped

1 red onion, chopped

6 cloves of garlic, crushed

2 green bell peppers, chopped

2 jalapeno peppers, chopped

¼ cup of lentils

4 diced tomatoes

2 tablespoons of chili powder

2 teaspoons of ground cumin

½ teaspoon of oregano

½ teaspoon of pepper

3 tablespoons of red wine vinegar

1 tablespoon of salt

½ cup of white rice

Method:

1. Chop and mince everything and them mix it all together in the slow cooker

2. Place on high heat and cook for about three hours

3. Serve and enjoy

Nutritional Information:

Calories: 231 kcal, Fats: 1.2 grams, Carbohydrates: 43.4 grams, Protein: 12.6 grams

Bowtie Pasta and Homemade Tomato Sauce

Ingredients:

10 plum tomatoes, peeled and crushed

½ of an onion, chopped

1 teaspoon of garlic, minced

¼ cup of olive oil

1 teaspoon of oregano

1 teaspoon of basil

1 teaspoon of cayenne pepper

1 teaspoon of salt

1 teaspoon of pepper

1 pinch of cinnamon

1 box of bowtie pasta

Method:

1. Peel and crush the tomatoes, mince the garlic and chop the onion

2. Place everything in the slow cooker and stir well

3. Cook on high for about four hours or so

4. Serve and enjoy

Nutritional Information:

Calories: 105 kcal, Fats: 9.3 grams, Carbohydrates: 5.5 grams, Protein: 1.2 grams

Rice Casserole

Ingredients:

2 onions, chopped

3 stalks of celery, sliced

4 ½ cups of mixed rice

2 ½ cups of water

1 can of mushroom soup

½ cup of butter

½ pound of shredded American cheese

½ cup of mushrooms, sliced

Method:

1. Chop everything up that needs to get cut and place in the slow cooker

2. Add everything else but the cheese in the slow cooker

3. Cook on high for about four hours

4. Serve and enjoy with the shredded cheese on top

Nutritional Information:

Calories: 408 kcal, Fats: 23 grams, Carbohydrates: 39.5 grams, Protein: 11.6 grams

Potato Soup

Ingredients:

1 onion, chopped

4 cups of chicken broth

2 cups of water

5 potatoes, diced

½ teaspoon of salt

½ teaspoon of dill weed

½ teaspoon of pepper

½ cup of all-purpose flour

2 cups of half and half cream

12 ounces of evaporated milk

Method:

1. Chop and dice everything that needs to get cut and combine all of the ingredients into the slow cooker

2. Cook on high heat for about three and a half hours

3. Serve and enjoy, try with some sour cream and some shredded cheese on top

Nutritional Information:

Calories: 553 kcal, Fats: 19.3 grams, Carbohydrates: 74.2 grams, Protein: 22 grams

Split Pea Soup

Ingredients:

1 pound of split peas

1 onion, chopped

3 carrots, chopped

3 stalks of celery, chopped

2 cloves of garlic, minced

1/8 teaspoon of pepper

1 pinch of red pepper flakes

8 cups of chicken broth

Method:

1. Chop everything up that needs to get cut and place all of the ingredients into the slow cooker

2. Cook on high heat for about five hours, stirring every so often

3. Serve and enjoy

Nutritional Information:

Calories: 273 kcal, Fats: 3.4 grams, Carbohydrates: 44 grams, Protein: 17.7 grams

Onion Soup

Ingredients:

6 tablespoons of butter

4 onions, sliced

1 tablespoon of white sugar

2 cloves of garlic, minced

½ cup of cooking sherry

7 cups of vegetable broth

1 teaspoon of salt

¼ teaspoon of thyme

1 bay leaf

8 slices of French bread

½ cup of shredded parmesan cheese

1/3 cup of shredded Colby jack cheese

¼ cup of cheddar cheese

2 tablespoons of mozzarella cheese

Method:

1. Chop everything up that needs to be cut and place in the slow cooker

2. Add in everything else but the cheese and the bread

3. Broil the bread in the oven for about three months

4. Place the slow cooker on high heat and cook for five hours

5. Serve and enjoy with some of the bread and the cheese on top

Nutritional Information:

Calories: 250 kcal, Fats: 14.7 grams, Carbohydrates: 17.5 grams, Protein: 11 grams

Zucchini Soup

Ingredients:

2 cups of chopped celery

2 pounds of zucchini, sliced

6 tomatoes, diced

2 green bell peppers, sliced

1 cup of chopped onion

2 teaspoons of salt

1 teaspoon of white sugar

1 teaspoon of oregano

1 teaspoon of Italian seasoning

1 teaspoon of basil

¼ teaspoon of garlic powder

6 tablespoons of shredded parmesan cheese

Method:

1. Chop up everything that needs to get cut up and place in the slow cooker except for the cheese
2. Stir well and put on high heat
3. Cook for about three and a half hours
4. Serve and enjoy with some of the shredded cheese on top

Nutritional Information:

Calories: 389 kcal, Fats: 23.6 grams, Carbohydrates: 25.8 grams, Protein: 21.8 grams

German Lentil Soup

Ingredients:

2 cups of brown lentils

3 cups of chicken broth

1 bay leaf

1 cup of carrots, chopped

1 cup of celery, chopped

1 cup of onion, chopped

1 teaspoon of Worcestershire sauce

½ teaspoon of garlic powder

¼ teaspoon of nutmeg

5 drops of hot sauce

¼ teaspoon of caraway seed

½ teaspoon of celery salt

1 tablespoon of parsley

½ teaspoon of pepper

Method:

1. Cut up everything that needs to get cut up

2. Place in the slow cooker and cook on high for about five hours

3. Remove the bay leaf

4. Serve and enjoy

Nutritional Information:

Calories: 221 kcal, Fats: 2.3 grams, Carbohydrates: 34.2 grams, Protein: 16 grams

Meatless Taco Soup

Ingredients:

1 onion, chopped

1 can of chili beans

1 can of kidney beans

1 can of corn

1 can of tomato sauce

2 cups of water

6 tomatoes, diced

2 green chili peppers

3 tablespoons of taco seasoning mix

Method:

1. Cut up everything that needs to be diced

2. Place in the slow cooker and stir well

3. Cook on high for about three and a half hours

4. Serve and enjoy, try with some sour cream and shredded cheese on top

Nutritional Information:

Calories: 362 kcal, Fats: 16.3 grams, Carbohydrates: 37.8 grams, Protein: 18.2 grams

Cabbage Soup

Ingredients:

2 tablespoons of vegetable oil

1 onion, chopped

5 cups of cabbage, chopped

2 cans of red kidney beans

2 cups of water

6 cups of tomato sauce

4 tablespoons of seasoned salt

1 ½ teaspoons of cumin

1 teaspoon of salt

1 teaspoon of pepper

Method:

1. Chop the cabbage and the onion up

2. Place in slow cooker with everything else

3. Cook on high for four hours

4. Serve and enjoy

Nutritional Information:

Calories: 211 kcal, Fats: 8.7 grams, Carbohydrates: 20.3 grams, Protein: 14.1 grams

Corn Chowder

Ingredients:

5 potatoes, peeled and cubed

2 onions, chopped

3 stalks of celery, chopped

1 can of whole kernel corn

2 tablespoons of butter

½ teaspoon of salt

½ teaspoon of pepper

2 tablespoons of seasoned salt

Method:

1. Peel and cube the potatoes

2. Chop the onions and the celery

3. Combine everything in the slow cooker

4. Set on high heat and cook for about four hours

5. Serve and enjoy

Nutritional Information:

Calories: 266 kcal, Fats: 8.8 grams, Carbohydrates: 37.8 grams, Protein: 11.2 grams

Tofu Curry

Ingredients:

1 pound tofu (firm; cubed)

2 cup sweet corn

15 oz coconut milk

¼ cup curry paste

2 cups vegetable stock

6 oz tomato paste (canned)

1 yellow pepper (chopped)

1 red pepper (chopped)

1 sweet onion (chopped)

3 garlic cloves (minced)

2 ginger (minced)

1 tbsp garam masala

1 tsp low salt

Cilantro (for garnishing)

Method:

1. Start by cutting the tofu into ½ inch cubes and add it to a large slow cooker.

2. Next add the chopped onion, peppers; ginger and garlic to the slow cooker as well followed by the corn, vegetable stock, tomato paste, coconut milk and spices.

3. Stir well! Then cover and allow the curry to cook on high heat for approximately 3 to 4 hours.

4. Serve over brown rice or as desired.

Nutritional Information:

Calories: 328 kcal, Fats: 7 grams, Carbohydrates: 53.8 grams, Protein: 12.8 grams

Some other recipe books for you to enjoy!

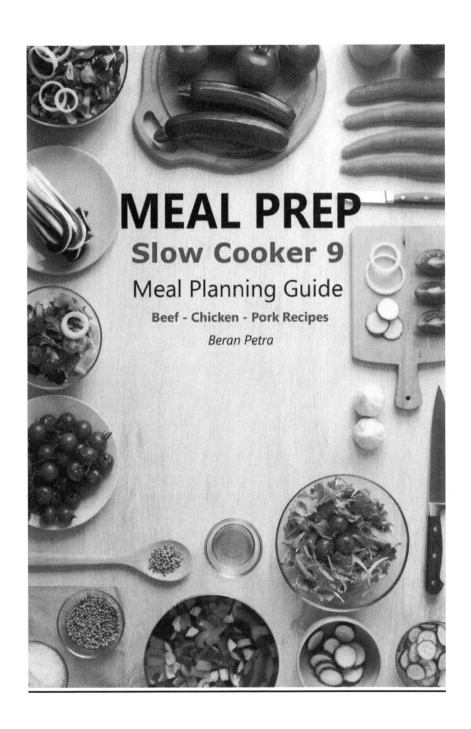

MEAL PREP
Slow Cooker 9
Meal Planning Guide

Beef - Chicken - Pork Recipes

Beran Petra

the best
Spice Mix
Recipes

Top 50 Seasoning Recipes

Olivia Rose / Recipe Junkies

DEXTER POIN

RICE

50+ RICE COOKER RECIPES

RICE

100% VEGAN APPROVED!

BABY

QUICK AND EASY COOKING FOR A HEALTHY WAY OF LIFE!

any treatment, action, application or preparation, to any person reading or following the information in this book. References are provided for informational purposes only and do not constitute endorsement of any websites or other sources. Readers should be aware that the websites listed in this book may change.

These recipes are not intended to be any type of Medical advice. ALL individuals must consult their Doctors first and should always receive their meal plans from a qualified practitioner. . These recipes are not intended to heal, or cure anyone from any kind of illness, or disease.

Made in the USA
Middletown, DE
04 December 2017